I hope you enjoy
it Julie
Love from

Derren xx

Walter K

Walter

Copyright

First published 2018 by Derren Riley.

ISBN: 978-1-5272-3405-5

ACKNOWLEDGEMENTS

This book would not have been possible without the efforts of so many.
To my 'Grumpy Hubby', aka Russ. I may annoy you and the three amigos and I may push your buttons to the limit, but you are amazing... just remember, dogs are like Mars bars; you can't just have one.

Also, to my lovely kids Sophie and Joe. I am proud of many things in my life but nothing beats you two.

Finally, to the wonderful people of Lytham and Homeward Bound. Without your help and support Walter may never have found his way home.

Derren, Nelly, Daisy and WALTER.

xx

About the author

Derren Leweson grew up in Lytham St Annes before marrying her long suffering husband Russell and taking on the name of RILEY.

She is mum to Sophie and Joe and her furbabies Nelly, Daisy and Walter.

By day she works in a local school but her true passion is animals.

Growing up was all about rescuing injured birds, stray dogs and cats, rehoming giant chickens and stopping her rabbits digging up her dad's prize garden, with her mum and sister as her accomplices.

Once married, the animals arrived in abundance and Russell slipped down the pecking order.

Welcome to the LIFE OF RILEY.

The legend begins...

The tale of Walter is not so much about a lanky legged racing machine, but how a lanky legged racing machine brought a little town together and helped form some special friendships along the way!

To understand how Walter captured everyone's heart, we need to go right back to the beginning.

I'd like to say that Walter was first noticed roaming the streets in December 2017, but it transpires that he was spotted in a garden in October and then again by my own daughter late at night in November, although we didn't know it was 'our' Walter.

Knowing what a total nutcase I am when it comes to animals my daughter rang me to tell me of her sighting and that the dog had sprinted off rapidly. Unfortunately, I was over 100 miles away at the time, so I could do very little but on my return the next morning my eyes were peeled... I could find neither hide nor hair though!

That brings us to freezing December nights. There had been lots of sightings of a lurcher/greyhound type dog racing at high speed down many main roads, avoiding traffic by the skin of his teeth and covering large areas of ground. With the help of 'Homeward Bound', a local volunteer group who give help and support for lost and found pets, a map was plotted of sightings; the area he covered was vast. Cars could be seen crawling along looking down side streets, people were openly looking and talking about the big dog that was running scared:

LYTHAM came alive to the needs of WALTER.

On the evening of Saturday 6th January 2018, a small army of volunteers were out in freezing conditions trying to catch this lanky sprinter. Despite being tracked down to Ansdell Institute on more than one occasion, he evaded us. We found what looked like his den; a tarpaulin rubbish dump. We left some food and arranged to meet at 6am the following morning.

The Capture: 7th January 2018

With temperatures dropping to -3° I couldn't sleep, and neither could other people. We met up as arranged and walked the streets. At his den, the food was gone but no dog. There were numerous sightings of him during the day and then the tables turned. He leapt over the wall at Lytham Hall right in front of me. What are the chances of this happening? He was not for sticking around though, and he sprinted off into 'Giggles Nursery' car park with me and my girls (two dogs, Daisy and Nelly) hobbling behind. The roast beef I'd carried round all week was in my car and the only things I had in my pocket were poo bags and treats. I threw the treats to him, which made my girls go bonkers, but he just bolted out onto Ballam Road. One car swerved to miss him and then the car coming in the opposite direction stopped, a girl jumped out and ran to keep up with the dog, with the car driver continuing to drive slowly along the road. The girl who was running was my daughter! Good job she's a runner.

She was joined by Lisa, one of the Homeward Bound volunteers, who had been following the story of the dog and together they chased him. Lots of local drivers were now desperately trying to help and the traffic was backed up. Picture the scene: cars zig zagging down Ballam Road with my daughter Sophie still running after him.

Eventually the dog was cornered in a garage and the chase was over.

We phoned ahead to let my husband know we had caught him and to put our girls out of the way so there was no trouble; after all this 'beast' had been roaming wild for a good while living out of bins and the last thing I wanted was for him to eat my dogs!!!

On arrival home the dog was scanned for a chip by Wendy Muleau, the founder of Homeward Bound, but nothing. It was noted that he was still entire - I hate that expression - not castrated and starving hungry. Under sufferance from my husband, it was decided (by ME) that we would hang on to him, as he was pathetically skinny and the thought of him going to some cold kennel (probably not cold - that's just my imagination) with a concrete floor was not happening. My husband went out to his golf club to cool off. I was so in the doghouse.

Ben, Sophie's boyfriend decided that this hound was going to be called Junior.

Finally, I am safe!

Safe!

The naming of the hound...

UPDATE... Name change - DODGER

'Junior' has settled really well. He has had a couple of small meals and is totally besotted with Sophie. Lytham is such a special place, with some totally amazing people. Junior is staying with us tonight and probably for the next few days whilst he relaxes from his ordeal; maybe longer if my marriage can withstand it.

This evening there was a family debate about Junior's name. As he had dodged traffic for so long, Ben was outnumbered; Junior became Dodger.

The beginning of Walter

Dodger doesn't suit his name. So, I polled family and friends asking for name suggestions. Wandering Walter won by a clear head. He started out as Junior, then Dodger and now he is firmly Walter.

He's been to the vet today and it appears he is about two years old, maybe younger. He's 5 - 6 kilos underweight, which indicates he's been feral for many weeks not just 3 or 4 days. My daughter is convinced this is the dog she followed in November, but he escaped her then as it was pitch black on Ballam Road.

Walter is desperate to be friends with my girls, Nelly a Tibetan Terrier and Daisy my crazy Cockapoo. Both are terrified of him as he's more like an antelope!

We are battling with the dog warden at the moment who wants to put Walter in kennels, rather than let him sleep on my bed as he is at the moment. We have told the warden that without a warrant, Walter is going nowhere. Not quite what I thought would happen but apparently, it's 'legislation'. Stuff legislation we say.

The love of Walter's new life is Sophie Riley. I think he sees her as his saviour. Odd really as she's wary of dogs, but Walter sits on her knee and follows her around constantly. He adores pinching her tuna fish whilst she makes her lunch for work. Fortunately for Walter, Sophie's boyfriend Ben is happy for him to sit between them on the settee.

As the days go on he is settling down and little bits of his personality are shining through. He's house-trained (phew), gentle and loves food. He doesn't know how to play and shouts at my girls if they play and try to involve him, so then they both hide. But, we had a breakthrough tonight;
he rested his head on Daisy the Cockapoo. She froze but it's a start.

For now though, he is happy, warm and safe.

And so it begins...

Walter has had a productive day today. This morning, Wendy from 'Homeward Bound' came around to my house to check up on him.

He's a little nervous so we are just taking it slowly but despite his nervous disposition, he's eating like a horse.

We have noticed over the past 24 hours that the tail that has been tucked away very tightly between his legs actually wagged a little. I'd like to say he was smiling too but then you'd all know I'm nuts!!!

We had a breakthrough with Daisy the Cockapoo this afternoon. She bravely climbed into Walter's bed with him. To be fair, I don't think she actually knew he was in there as he lays very still and is so thin you can't really see him. He sat up and she stayed in with him for about 30 seconds but it's a start.

Still no updates on the legal side of things but my theory is 'no news is good news'.

Nelly being brave whilst Walter's not looking

OMG! I didn't think you were in here.

Foibles

Small characteristics are coming through with Walter. He hates laminate floors and has become a bit of a prima donna in the morning. He categorically refuses to leave his bed until one of us slides his bed across the bedroom floor to reach the carpeted landing, where he happily trots out of bed and goes downstairs.

We had to leave him and the girls on their own for 2 hours today. I knew the girls were fine, but I wasn't sure if Walter would be distressed or worse, eat my house. However, no worries on that score; fast asleep in his bed and my house was still intact.

At lunch time I made cheese on toast. Little did we know how much Walter loves cheese! Whilst my girls might sit looking at me longingly for a piece, Walter can reach the worktop and pinch the cheese without shame and lick his lips in the process.

He's relaxing a little and even tried to play today, although he made a total hash of it. Daisy the Cockapoo was jumping all over him when suddenly Walter put his 'arm' round her. She froze, and she sat there thinking 'what do I do now?' Eventually Daisy unravelled herself, went and got a reindeer chew and shared it with him.

Our walk was short and sweet today. Walter is sporting a waterproof jacket that we feel makes him look like Count Dracula, but it keeps him warm and cosy.

Priced up fence panels today to put on top of our six foot walls. Hopefully Walter can then go out in the garden on his own without dragging me to every bush for a wee. Don't boy dogs go a lot? We daren't let him out on his own but, to be honest, I actually think he knows which side his bread's buttered, because as soon as he's done it's straight back inside to his bed next to the radiator.

Sporting my new coat
'Count Dracula'

Treat time at
the zoo

Three Reindeer chews
saved Daisy

And sleep zzzzz

Result

A short update today but nevertheless GOOD NEWS. We have only heard this second-hand but apparently the dog warden has wished Walter well. Also, Radio Lancashire wants to run the Walter story. I have spoken to them today, but we are deferring any story until Walter has served his 28 days with us and I have recovered from the flu enough to stop coughing. Considering how long this lanky sprinter stayed out in the cold it's hard to imagine how he survived. He can't get close enough to radiators, fires and people. He really is just a gentle giant.

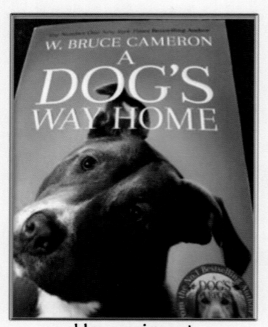

How poignant

How bizarre is this?
One of my Christmas presents from my husband got lost and decided to turn up today. Very apt at the moment and even the picture on the front cover is similar; funny how things turn out.

Home improvements

Today's been a B&Q day. Despite grotty weather, my lovely husband has been and bought the fence panels and heightened our garden walls so that Walter the gazelle can't leap over them. A man wouldn't be a man if he didn't moan the whole way through it, but it's finished now. In the meantime, my son, who is now Walter's new best mate, took Walter out for a run on the green.

This afternoon the girls, Walter and I went mud sliding in Witch Wood.

Everything was going great until a squirrel decided to come down a tree in front of me.

I gripped the lead, expecting the worst, thinking 'OMG, how will I stay upright', then Daisy sprinted off, whilst Walter stood perfectly still looking at me as if to say, 'how ridiculous is she!'. Walter didn't move! However, when we got to the Ansdell end of the wood, his nose went up in the air and I think if he hadn't been on a lead he may have run off. Very strange behaviour.

We've waited all evening for the sign he wanted to go outside, and we've just had it. He's been outside off the lead, although hubby and I escorted him just in case we had to rugby tackle him off the wall. No need to worry; quick wee and straight back in the warm and upstairs waiting to go to bed. There's still no way will he walk on the laminate floor, so my husband not only slid him across the floor in his bed but has laid towels down as a runner, so he's not trapped. Obviously, my husband doesn't want him here. He is softer than me.

Baby steps are getting bigger.

I'm NOT walking on
that floor

Nice... I totally love the
heat. Roll on summer

Life is great with cuddles

Today the inevitable happened

I decided to take a leap of faith with Walter and give him the opportunity to walk on his training lead rather than his short slip lead. It's not very easy walking three totally unruly nutcases, but we manage. I should have realised I was making a mistake; Walter, who usually walks OK, was bunny hopping down Ballam Road full of beans. Nelly and Daisy were released in Witch Wood and Walter was given 15m of slack. He was good and kept coming back for treats when I called him. After an hour, and with all three dogs muddy, we left the woods and decided to go over a very boggy and muddy Park View. The girls were released again, and Walter was switched to a long lead. Then it happened. Walter decided he wanted to play too. At least I think he was playing. He might have been trying to eat Nelly and Daisy might have been trying to pull him off! Suddenly Walter took off like Shergar. The only problem with that was that he was still tied to me. I faceplanted in the mud, but to his credit Walter did come back for a biscuit when I hollered at him. Muddy me and three out of control filthy dogs made a hasty retreat home.

HELP!

I have developed a problem. Walter will not walk on any laminate floors. We only have two in the house: initially it was my bedroom (being carpeted in Feb, so not too worried about that one) but now it's our kitchen too. He won't come in for food or to go out in the garden. This has developed over the past 24 hours. Initially we were amused but now we realise we have a problem. We have laid towels across the floor, but I can't live like this.

Update

WALTER 1: RILEYs 0

So, my house is now just a mass of carpets. Thanks to my lovely friend Sandra, who's just had a carpet fitted, we've got the off cuts and Walter has tentatively been making moves around the kitchen.

First walk on the 'red' carpet

Mat madness

And more…

Pamper party time

We've been out for a monster walk today in the gorgeous sunshine for a change. Walter was as good as gold except that we met another greyhound type dog and he tried to hump it. It was a male dog, so not only does he have issues with the floor, he's developing some other odd tendencies too. I need to get him castrated and soon.

He's been pampered this afternoon. He was offered a pamper from Kate Daley and Michelle Camp at Wags, but they both involved taking him away from home to their beauty salons and it was too soon for that. Nelly and Daisy have a monthly groom by Brenda at Best Buddy's and she comes to us. So, with me in the van, we (I just watched) gave Walter what I can only assume was his first ever pamper party and he totally loved it. Brenda trimmed his nails and hey ho, he trotted into the kitchen and then remembered he didn't like the floor. But he is a little better in that respect. We've picked up some carpet and we're using sausages to entice him to walk across the floor. The girls love this sausage trail game.

Let's see what tomorrow brings, can't wait.

Omg I'm not sure about this

What's going on?

Pamper party time

All clean and beautiful

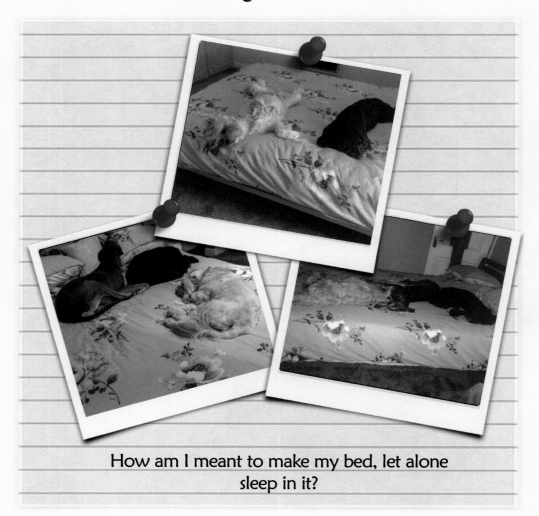

How am I meant to make my bed, let alone
sleep in it?

Move over

I am free to speak now

As it was Christmas time, the dog warden was closed, so we opted to keep Walter. However, three days later, when the office re-opened, the warden phoned to tell us that Walter HAD to go into kennels - it was the law. Now the lanky legged racing machine had not only started to relax but had made a massive dent in the 'Riley' hearts. We refused to let him go. Many phone calls, emails and a lot of unnecessary upset culminated with us being told that Walter would be seized, to which we retaliated with 'not without a warrant'. Lytham was put on standby in case someone tried to grab the gentle giant but thankfully the warden backed down and we were given a 28-day finder's permit. If no one claimed him within that 28 days, we had to send an email stating we would keep him.

So, today is Walter's release date. We've had him 28 days today and believe that means he is now ours. We won!!!

Welcome to the Riley mad house.

My forever home

Jittery

Poor old Walter has not had a good day today. He got up this morning and was in a very nervous state. Nothing particular had happened but his disposition was very submissive. With lots of cuddles and support his little tail uncurled and he relaxed. By the time of our afternoon walk he was much better but then unfortunately on the walk by Fairlawn, he was attacked by not just one dog, but two! Both were Cocker Spaniels and owned by different people.

Walter was walking beautifully on his lead when the first dog came over sniffed him then went for him big style. I held on for grim death as he tried frantically to run praying his collar wouldn't slip off.

Eventually the other owner got his dog, apologised and walked off. My priority was a very distressed Walter. Then, damn me, another then went for him. Walter showed not one ounce of aggression, just total fear and for the next 20 minutes he was glued to the spot shaking. He wouldn't move; biscuits, encouragement and cuddles had no effect.

Eventually, we managed to set off for home but with one jelly (Walter), one nutcase (Daisy) and one disgruntled terrier (Nelly), it was easier said than done. I'm struggling to walk three dogs but on days like today it's nigh on impossible!

Walter is so sad tonight, even Daisy can't work her magic.

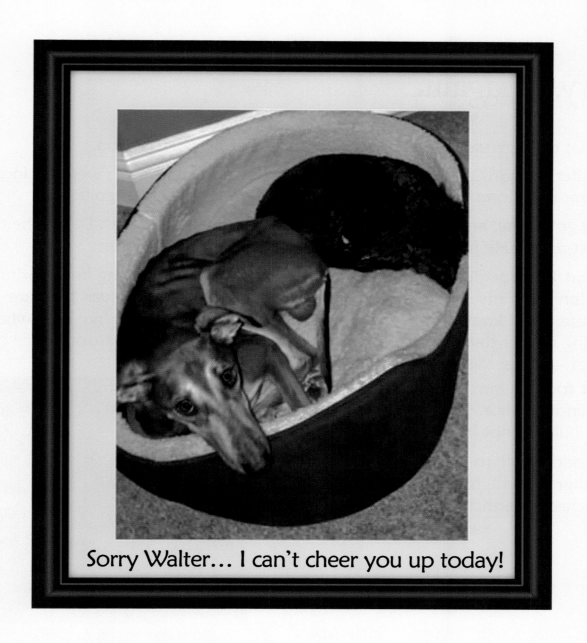

Sorry Walter… I can't cheer you up today!

Try, try again...

What do they say if you fall off your bike? Get straight back on.

Walter, the girls and I went for a nice muddy walk and there were no incidents. I kept him close; no long leads today and he was as good as gold.

We got home, and he went back to playing in the garden with Daisy albeit being a bit rough. He made her cry but still she went back for more!

Roast Beef for dinner tonight. Now when the electric carving knife springs into action both my girls charge into the kitchen from where ever they are in the house; they know I'm a soft touch. Walter had absolutely no idea what was going on but started jumping up and down like a giant kangaroo. A slice of beef each - I swear Walter was grinning.

Just to keep him smiling, I gave them all another slice. Six slices down; hope my hubby's not hungry!

To add insult to injury, not only has Walter eaten hubby's dinner, he's pinched his armchair too.

Nice dinner, nice chair...

Boys will be boys; not for much longer Walter!

I had to take the gang (can't say girls anymore) for an earlier than usual walk as I'm off to London with my son for a very important meeting. Everything was going great 'ish', until we met up with Bella, a lovely Springer Spaniel. Before having Walter, the girls and I walked with Bella and her mum on numerous occasions. Today however, Bella was with her Dad. We said good morning and he went his way and I tried to go mine. Wrong! Walter was pulling like crazy to get to Bella. Bella and her owner, oblivious to my dilemma with a frantic Walter, walked away and then doubled back on themselves along another path. Walter, being a 'sight hound', spotted her and we took off at a rapid speed smashing into trees and bushes on route. I am now sportingvarious cuts to my face and a fresh bruise to my eye. I look like a cage fighter. My meeting will be conducted in a Jackie O state with sunglasses.

Anyway, back to Walter. In the sugar coated world I live in, I decided that in a former life Walter had a 'friend' like Bella and he was getting confused. This made me sad as I imagined him missing his friend. I explained to Bella's dad why we raced at him through the undergrowth and we walked on together chatting, with Walter dragging me through the mud. After about 10 minutes and with arms now six inches longer, a massive Golden Retriever bounded up to Bella andimmediately started to hump her. Bella's dad jumped into action and pushed the dog off. The Retriever's lady owner asked if Bella was in season and the man said no but she had just finished. Then the penny dropped. Bella wasn't like an old long-lost friend to Walter; she was humping material. My little illusion was shattered.

Guess what? Walter is being castrated on Monday!

Off to the vets. Not happy!

Job done

I'm writing this with Walter asleep on the carpet. Today has been a tough one (for him, not me). He's been castrated!

He jumped out of bed as normal and raced downstairs for his breakfast. As he was nil by mouth, I didn't think it fair to feed the girls either, so I had three fed up mutts. When he realised they weren't coming on the car journey he dug his heels in, not wanting to get in the car. With a lot of persuasion, he finally got in. My fabulous vet, Greenways, were awaiting his arrival and after signing the consent form I left with the sound of Walter howling in the background. Didn't bode well as they hadn't touched him at that point.

3pm collection time. Walter wasn't exactly over the moon to see me because of the anaesthetic, but I think he hates me for removing his manhood. The lovely Zoe explained how she'd had quite a hard job as he has a very large scrotum (yuck) and there was lots of blood, so she had to put double stitches in but not to worry if tomorrow he gets up and his sack has filled to the size of a grapefruit with blood. Well that's something to look forward to; not!

Who knew five weeks ago my life would be so much fun?

30

Normal service has been resumed!

Poor Walter! Last night he was bruised, battered and miserable. However, today he is back on track. After a lie in this morning we decided not to pander to his pathetic crying any longer. His nether region is reducing in size and Daisy is not so fixated on the new ball that appears to be attached to him. This morning it was a full-on sprint around the garden after Daisy who hid in a holly bush until he wasn't looking, then dived out, punched him in the head and ran off.

My hubby has taken him for a short walk this afternoon and now appreciates how strong he is after they met men in hi vis jackets. I'd probably have ended up in Southport.

Walter's play date

I'm not too sure who had the best day; me, Walter or maybe Daisy. I'd arranged to meet a variety of different sized dogs at Lowther Gardens at 1.30pm. I took the three amigos to Witch Wood to let them run some energy off first.

We met at 1:30pm as arranged at Lowther Gardens tennis court after an hour's walk through Witch Wood knee deep in mud. Oh my goodness, it's so slippery at the moment. The girls raced about like the total nutcases they are, and Walter walked beautifully. I've bought a Halti for both him and Daisy. Walter took to it like a dream whilst Daisy insists on doing the alligator roll at every given moment and somehow manages to get the thing in her mouth. To be fair, I think they will be my saving grace.

I'd like to say a massive 'thank you' to all the lovely ladies and pooches who arrived to entertain Walter. There was an array of sizes from tiny Lucy to bear size Belle.

Walter ran with a ball for the first time - that's progress. And he didn't attempt to eat any dog presented to him - very encouraging. His recall is shady (non-existent really) but the sausages helped a little. I'd like to say he's learning his name but I'm not 100% sure.

I'd definitely like to meet again soon for another play date but for now the dogs are pooched!

Pooched!

Weary, very weary

33

Lovely Bella

One of the nicest things about finding Walter is the fabulous people I've met and like to say made friends with. Today We walked through Witch Wood with Julia who doesn't own a dog but fell in love with Walter and his story. She messaged me to ask if she could join us on a walk and today she took charge of Walter!

Everything was going great guns until the flirtatious Bella (remember Friday and the drag through bushes dog) appeared. I have no idea what it is about that dog, but Walter became a quivering wreck and it wasn't through fear! OMG he is totally loved up. Bella, being the 'tart', she is, lay on the floor with her legs in the air! Julia, Bella's lovely owner and I were giggling at these antics; unlike last time, I was able to pull Walter away. I'm guessing his urges aren't as strong now he's carrying a 'bit-less' in the nether regions. He cried for about a minute until it became 'out of sight out of mind' and off to the park we went.

Mud, mud, glorious (or not so glorious) mud!

The past two days have been very busy in the Riley household. My husband went away on Wednesday and I had a cunning plan in place. All very sneaky. I've painted furniture, arranged for a new carpet (Walter still doesn't like laminate flooring; expensive dog this one) and had a decorator in to paper the ceiling.

I went to work yesterday and when I got home my house was covered in mud. I don't do dirt. My settee was filthy; my window sill black; my carpets grubby and my paintwork splattered. I could not work out why! Then the decorator informed me he'd let the dogs out to play in the garden all morning. Oh no! The garden. OMG. My husband will go mental. The lawn has vanished, and we now have a race track. Hubby will kill me! I told the decorator to be very careful with Walter or we'll lose him. And what did he do? He let Walter out!

Then Walter decided the post looked tasty. Despite the mail being put in a letter box with a lid, Walter decided to lift the lid and eat the Motability catalogue. How much mess can this dog with monster feet and teeth make? I know what I'll be up to this weekend: cleaning, gardening (mahoosive job) and decorating. I might have to pay for my husband to stay away for six months.

Nelly's night

Wow! It's been chilly today but not too chilly for our Walter. Up at the crack of dawn and straight out into the snow, rolling in it and charging round with 'devil dog' Daisy in close pursuit. The lawn looked OK with a white blanket covering it but now it looks a muddy wreck.

Hubby is back tomorrow so I think my life span is quite short now! Nelly is poorly, very sick and out of sorts, so no walk for the gang today. I will pay the price later when they are both hyper at bedtime, but Nelly is my priority today.

Last night was entertaining. We have a cuckoo clock in our lounge and I wound it up without even thinking about Walter. At 5:30pm it cuckooed once and Walter was out of his bed looking for the mystery sound. At 6pm it was chaos. Racing through the house barking (Walter doesn't bark and when he does the windows shake!!!); he went berserk. It's a clock you goon. However, by 6:30pm the cuckoo had been locked in his house - can't put up with that. This evening we are all snuggled up with the fire on watching TV and taking care of lovely Nelly.

Poorly Nelly

The wanderer returns

Well he's home and fortunately the lawn is hidden under a dusting of snow, so I live to write another update about our lovely Walter.

Despite arctic conditions, we went for a 'brisk' walk. It's hard to imagine Walter living rough at all when you see what a pampered prince he has become. Coat and HALTI on and Daisy in close pursuit. Nelly is still out of sorts, but a bit better, so she stayed at home. The three musketeers - me and two dogs stepped out of the front door and Walter sat down and looked at me as if to say, 'you have got to be mad, I'm not taking you out in this'. Actually, I'm taking you Walter. Daisy is just happy to be alive and raring to go.

A quick lap of Witch Wood, nose running, eyes streaming (I'm sure my eye sockets are too big for my eyes) and home. Walter virtually dragged me home. He knows the place to be and it's not outside! During his dinner I noticed that he has licked his castration scar raw. On closer inspection and trying to get an antelope to lie on his back with his legs in the air is not easy, it looks like one of the stitches has gone yucky. Not wanting to hurt him but very tempted to squeeze to see if anything came out, I opted for plan B; pants on. Joe's baby knickers were too small and pinched into other vital man parts, so my daughter Sophie's smalls were stolen from her room. Thongs definitely not suitable, so 'Bridget Jones' it is. I put them on a most indignant Walter only for devil dog Daisy to whip them off and play tug of war. I can feel a vet trip coming on this weekend. I'll keep you posted how we get on.

BTW, the decorating is finished and my new bedroom looks fab. Well Walter thought it was comfy last night! Sleep rough? Who me?

38

Brief encounter

I know he's back but let us out.

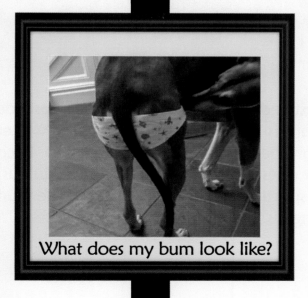

What does my bum look like?

Knickers!

Just returned from the vets with Walter due to his 'yucky' scar! The good news is he has put four kilos on in weight in the short time we've had him. He eats like a horse so I'm not too surprised.

Unfortunately, the vet, a locum, was completely unaware of Walter's history. I can only assume he has lived under a rock for the past month.

He was a little unsympathetic to his wary disposition. I think he might have been a little stressed too, (the vet, not Walter). He asked me to lift Walter's front legs onto the table. Now I'm a dainty 5ft 2inch, so lifting an uncooperative antelope was not easy. However, I had a plan. I had a biscuit that I held up, so he put his paws on my shoulder and hey ho, the vet could slide underneath  him. One quick look and Walter was destined to wear the biggest lampshade you've ever seen and have antibiotics. There is no way we could subject Walter to that, especially as Daisy would probably be scooped up in it too, so Tesco here I come! Star Wars pants were the only ones I could get, £6 a pair (ridiculous) with a hole for his tail and he is sporting them with pride. He just needs a light sabre now. We will be removing his 'draws' when out in public.

'Stars Wars' all the way

Scary stuff

Today has been a seaside day. Walter has been paddling. I'm a little unsure about Walter's behaviour over the past two days.

Yesterday we (hubby and me) took all the dogs on the tennis courts by our house. Walter has now taken to chasing a ball. My God I now know why he took so long to catch; he is rapid. However, devil dog Daisy isn't as daft as she looks and raced through Walter's legs and got the ball first. He was not happy. Next thing we knew, Daisy was being lifted off the floor. Unfortunately, we were not close enough to see if it was by her neck or if his monster teeth had become caught in her HALTI. It made no difference, I yelled at him and reduced him to a gibbering jelly. Daisy lay motionless on the floor, but her tail was wiggling a little bit. Nelly couldn't have cared less.

This has unnerved me a little!

Oh no

Today I took them to Lowther Gardens and although he didn't lift her up, he did put her head in his mouth and I know she wasn't too keen. My heart stopped.

Off to the beach next so the girls could have a good old run, only Walter wanted to paddle too. Unfortunately, they are banned from the garden as a group to try and salvage the grass. So individual wees allowed only.

One thing I have to remember though is to remove Walter's knickers before he goes for a poo.

'Yogi bear'

Today has been Walter's big test. When I say big, nothing major, just mixing with big dogs, or rather bigger than Daisy and Nelly dogs. We met Yogi, who I have to say is probably the biggest dog I've ever seen. Walter wasn't phased in the slightest and Daisy thought he was great, even if he did keep chasing her. I think she gives off that air of 'chase me, chase me'! And they do. Nelly, being the calm one of the three, just kept chasing her ball.

Yogi

Nelly: I love Yogi

We were joined by Sue and Lucy dog who, despite being tiny, has obviously hit a soft spot with Walter as he swoons over her. We had spectators to watch the play date in the form of Walter's grandparents (my mum and dad) who enjoyed watching him stretch his legs a bit but were concerned by the very deep rumble he gave off as he tried to swallow Daisy. At nearly 90 years of age they didn't stay long as it was chilly, but they've seen him in action now.

Walter meet Yogi

Hi Yogi, I'm Daisy

45

Drowning dog

I'm still shaking with the adrenaline after today's walk! A beautiful day, so I thought we'd have a change of scenery: Lytham Hall here we come. We cut across Park View, the girls running like maniacs, Walter desperate to, but no way was he being allowed off his lead! Then into Lytham Hall. We walked all over it to see if there was anywhere that was secure enough for me to chance it with Walter but unfortunately not. With the sun shining, we took a moment to enjoy the view and with Walter crying pathetically I felt like a really bad mum restraining him all the time, however needs must. Collecting the numerous poo bags, we set off for our next destination; Witch Wood. The girls had other ideas though. There's a small, very deep lake at Lytham Hall and Nelly fell in. Not sure how it happened but she was clinging to a log. I couldn't get a photo; her life was in the balance. Daisy was bouncing on one end of the log. I'd like to think she was doing that to alert me but in reality, I think it was to wobble the log so Nelly would fall in. I swear I could see Walter laughing. Despite trying to entice her, Nelly was stuck! Tying Walter to a post and with Daisy licking my face, I lay down to grab Nelly by the collar, only for her to jump out and shake all over me!

B****** dogs!

Next stop was Witch Wood and thankfully it was uneventful in there which gave me time to compose myself for the next hurdle.

Do I or don't I let Walter off on Park View?

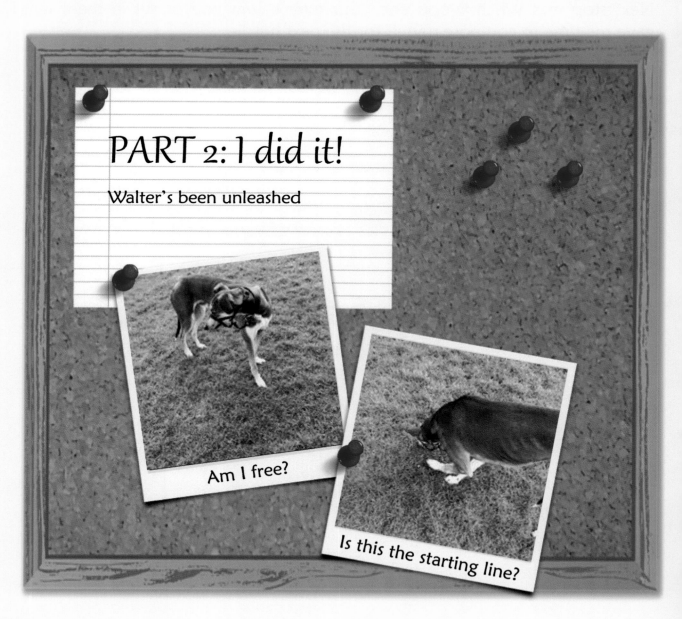

PART 3: The proof

I need a lie down and a stiff drink (me, not Walter).

Party time again

The 'big' dog party continued for Walter today thanks to Fiona and Dave bringing their Lurchers Bramley and Red to the tennis courts. We bumped into them all in Lytham first and Walter was a little apprehensive. Something we've not really seen before, however, with a careful introduction, everything was perfect and Walter's very happy disposition shone through. He really is such a gentle baby and everyday he just gets more and more loving. He thrives on cuddles, kisses and hugs. To try and envisage his former life is impossible. If he was bred for coursing, I can only assume his personality got him sacked.

He was desperate to get back on Park View to stretch his legs today, but as there was a little boys' football match going on, he was not let off. I didn't think a long-legged lanky antelope in the middle of the pitch would go down too well, so we kept away. We did make up for it though on the tennis courts and finally on the beach.

It's quite incredible how such a big dog gets so tired after a couple of hours exercise. So, to get home and find his mate here (my son Joe) was a real bonus.

Mother's day

Mother's Day started with a punch in the eye from Walter. It's great sharing your bed with three dogs but oh, there is so little room. It's not been the relaxing day I was hoping for as I thought I'd give Walter a Mother's Day run. I took him on St Bede's school field and warily let him off, only for him to run a little, stop, lift his head to the sky and promptly leap over the school fence like a horse in the Grand National. My heart literally stopped. I called his name, very loudly, and he jumped back over the fence and came back to me cowering. Obviously not nice to see him scared but OMG we have progress; he came back. Now do I put him on his lead or let him keep his freedom? I opted for freedom. I gave him a treat for coming back and then let him have a bit more of a run with Daisy.

My nerves are shot to pieces; red wine required.

Steps

I've worked out that Walter must have done about 60,000 steps today. After all he has four legs. It probably explains why he's collapsed in the chair snoring like a pig.

Divorce pending

At the moment I'm sat on the tennis courts at Lowther Gardens with three loony dogs, one who is destined for death row! We've been walking the streets for hours due to an incident that had happened at home.

We need to buy a Walter Fitbit

Just when I thought I'd won my husband round, despite his beautiful lawn, the hound has gone one massive leap further; he's chewed my leather settee. I came downstairs this morning to see the arm had a hole in it. My life expectancy gets shorter by the minute! In full panic, I threw a coat over the evidence, but I knew coming clean was the only option. I wanted to throw Walter in the garden but that's a no no too. Blimey it's hard in the Riley residence.

Anyone want a dog? Or better still, three dogs?

Floored

The sun was shining when we set off for our daily walk but I was convinced that it would be dark by the time I got home.

Lytham Hall was beautiful with Nelly and Daisy belting through the trees - two happy girls and Walter trotting along beside me. Witch Wood - similar scenario. Park View? Oh, Park View - how very different. Everyone (dog wise) was relaxed, so getting cocky, I let Walter off; off being the operative word. Two seconds rolling around the floor with Daisy and his legs took over. He went into sprint mode, round and round, and round he raced. That's it he's gone and then, I can only say that Johnny Wilkinson should sign me up for rugby, I took him out. Three broken nails later and he's back under control. My heart said he would come back but my body black and blue as it is, now says he won't!

Thank God!
Tesco has just delivered more wine.

Good morning

Too good to be true! I should have known this photo first thing was the calm before the storm.

After a tough morning I needed my fresh air fix. Me and the gang set off to Lytham Hall. A heron flew overhead and landed in a nest just above my head by the lake. Totally transfixed I was oblivious to the fact Daisy was swimming after two ducks who only alerted me by quacking loudly and splashing about. Daisy was having a ball and thought this was a great game. When she finally came back to shore she stank! She is a total nightmare. Nelly and Walter were perfect, and I even braved letting Walter off his lead for a 10-minute wander around the garden.

We went to Witch Wood where we met up with Digby the rescue Labrador puppy. Everyone was getting on great - a bit of a 'party in the park' until recently castrated Digby let the side down by trying to mount Nelly. Although she is more than capable of putting everyone in their place, Walter took the role of big brother and told Digby off. It was actually nice to see, no aggression; just a very loud bark but enough to make me jump and enough to frighten poor Digby. Play date arranged on Tuesday for Walter, Digby and any other friends to meet up and put their differences aside.

Onto Park View for what has now become a regular run. Each day Walter is getting faster and faster. Thankfully after about four laps of the park he collapses in a heap panting as though it's his last breath. To be honest though I don't think his heart is racing as much as mine. He has come back though, so that's a bonus. I know it's a school night, but I need alcohol. I blame Walter for my addiction.

Bushed

Gardening

Today has been all about gardening and sun bathing.

I was up early as we have workmen in the house, so the dogs were on an early walk around our usual route. Lytham Hall was stunning at 9am - peaceful and quiet. We followed on with Witch Wood where Walter saw from afar, the love of his life, Bella! Ears pert, not to mention other bits and with a definite smile upon his face, he trembled his way over to Bella who promptly lay on her back with her legs in the air. Tart! After a quick sniff (so polite) I can only assume testosterone (think that's spelt right) must be subsiding as he did a quick jump in the air and left Bella horizontal in the dirt.

Then we were off to Park View for a morning sprint. We couldn't do it over the weekend as a man with four chihuahuas was on the park and I was worried Walter would eat them. So much pent up energy today but after the obligatory four laps he collapsed in a heap!

Finally, home where my husband was tending his lawn; seeding, rolling, virtually cuddling it. Too nice to be indoors but too risky to let them out. I know, I'll butter him up! I asked, 'would you like a cuppa?' He replied, 'yes, but don't let the dogs out' Damn! That didn't work. I made the tea, opened the kitchen door and they all escaped. Total carnage. As you can imagine, I'm back in the doghouse.

Idea! I went and got Walter's bed and put it in the garden.

Yes, sunbathing was on his agenda; he loves the sun. I lay on a lounger and relaxed, but not for long. Walter totally loves me, 'Let's share the lounger Mum.'

I now have crushed lungs.

My 'BIG' baby xx

The calm before the storm!

So, today has been a full-on day but nice nevertheless. Started with a smack in the face from Walter at 6:05 am. Good job really as I was having my hair cut at 9am and the hounds needed their breakfast.

At the hairdressers, we carried out an experiment with curly hair (on me not one of the hounds!). Joe did a poll on Instagram and the results are:

- 970 people prefer it curly
- 379 prefer it straight

Funny really when I've no idea who any of these voters are.

Went out for lunch with my kids. I know they are buttering me up, but it left me feeling mellow and cocky.

Then it was out with the beasts. Normally (but today isn't a normal day) I'd walk down Ballam Road and then let Walter free for the last 10 minutes on Park View, but not today. I set off across Park View and immediately let Walter off. He stopped, looked at me as if to say, 'this isn't the way we do it', then he sprinted off before I could change my mind. A quick circuit and then straight back to me for a wild boar treat. Then we moved off to Witch Wood where Daisy caused her normal chaos with the smart Saturday shoppers; jumping all over them. One day someone will punch her.

After Witch Wood we trotted off to the back of Fairlawn. Hmmm decision: high wall one side, chain link fence the other. Should I try new territory? Hey ho, why not? Bit stupid of me really. Everything was going great until Nelly brought me her ball to throw, as she does. Obviously, I threw it and Walter was off. B******, I'd forgotten I'd let him off! He grabbed the ball and was off, heading in the direction of Southport. Out of sight now, I presumed he was a gonna; but wait - there's a dot speeding my way. It was Walter. He came back and collapsed at my feet. An elderly couple who were leisurely strolling behind stopped and commented on his amazing recall, 'if only all dogs were as well behaved,' they said. Little did they know! I'm shakily putting Walter's lead back on and pretending I'd no idea who Daisy belonged to!

Back to Park View again but there was a football match in play so no run about. Perhaps it's just as well as tonight, my kids, 21 & 22, are having a 'gathering'. I've never seen so much alcohol! I've been making punch - the strongest stuff I've ever tasted and Pornstar Martini (very moreish).
In fact, I've drunk the first batch; purely in the name of research you understand.

My only concern is… well I have two actually:

1. the door is left open and Walter wanders: Lytham be on standby; or

2. Walter mines sweeps the spillage from the floor and ends up drunk as a skunk.

Very moreish!

'Bee' have

Walter's had an encounter today and unfortunately, he came off worse! I'd like to say we had a leisurely walk but with Daisy that's impossible. Swimming in Lytham Hall, diving in every ditch where ducks are resting and generally being a total nightmare and Daisy's recall is non-existent when she meets fellow Cockapoos. You have to understand that this is extremely embarrassing when the other dog walks to heel and Daisy is trying to grab the treats out of the other owner's pocket. Thief. However, Nelly, the love of my life, is just sucking on her ball waiting for life to return to normal. Well that's never going to happen.

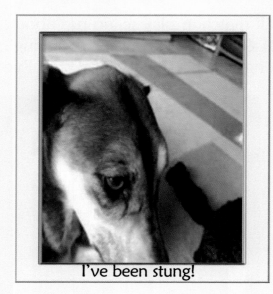
I've been stung!

As usual we went off to Park View where lovely Walter met his attacker... a huge bumble bee. After pouncing on it, said bee tried to fly away but Walter went for the kill. But no way was that bee going down without a fight and of course it stung Walter on the nose. OMG it was like someone pressed the eject button; he was off. The circles he had been doing went out of the window and he was in full flight! Despite the bile in my throat, I blew our whistle. Not sure how many times I blew it, but he came back. I had to lie down on the grass; yes, it was wet, but I didn't care!

Now that was the scariest session so far ... my heart can't take much more.

Home to rest and guess what? WINE!

Not a good day in the RILEY house today

I am truly questioning if we've done the right thing with Walter.
We love him to bits but...

I took my hubby to Dobbies Garden Centre today to try and placate him with replacement shrubs, only to return home to find not only has Walter eaten our new lounge armchair but worse still it's Russ' chair. He has also eaten the TV remote and now the TV doesn't work. There are only so many battles I can fight for this dog and I'm battle weary!

Positivity

All positive today after a major wobble yesterday.

The three musketeers and I had a fab walk today. We met up with Snoop, Nelly's best mate, on the back of Fairlawn and I, with a different dog in the group, made the decision to let Walter go; he was great. He had the obligatory sprint but came back, much to my relief. Snoop's mum, Shirley, was very impressed with his speed, 'like a race horse,' she said. I think he's like a cheetah.

On to the beach for a paddle next. Walter loved it. Eventually we rolled home where we all collapsed in a heap... exhausted.

I've found a man to repair my sofa(s). Bless him. Walter not the repair man. Something to do with wax, glue and paint. Roll on next Wednesday when it might be fixed. eBay have very kindly replaced my TV remote. So, all is good - just a bit more out of the bank account.

Good old Walt. Can't help it. I adore lanky legs xx

Miracle Man

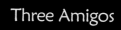

Three Amigos

Sweet dreams

Last night at bed time Walter was told to sleep in his bed. He's so big and heavy, and he takes up so much room on my bed. He settled down and so did I, and finally I fell into a really deep sleep.

But at 2am Walter had other ideas about me having a really long night's sleep. He got out of his bed and trotted round to my side, stood with his nose centimetres from my face and barked. One very loud bark. OMG, he frightened the living daylights out of me. He then climbed up on my bed snuggled down and within minutes was snoring like a trooper. He is one pampered pooch.

Walter has had an appointment at the vet today. Unfortunately, some of his castration stitches haven't dissolved and they are like barbed wire in his nether region, hence why he has been licking so much. This is the excuse I'm using for him eating my furniture!

Whilst at the vet I met a lovely couple, Mr. & Mrs. Langley, who had a cat. Now Walter has never met a cat and all I've heard about lurchers and cats are horror stories. The lovely lady said her cat was dog friendly, but I explained I had no idea how Walter would react. But he was perfect - no reaction at all. It transpired that her husband was one of the original Walter hunters. It's a small world.

In to see lovely Fiona, the vet, who removed most of Walter's stitches, with him and me lying on the floor having a cuddle. My part was easy. Out of the consultation room and off to pay the bill. Lots of those this week - cheers Walt! Mrs. Langley in front of me paid her bill and left. The only problem was she unknowingly 'stole' my drugs. I waited and waited but no drugs. Then we realised what had happened. The lovely Auntie Jan on reception phoned her and we giggled when I told her I'd name and shame on Facebook.

Only joking. Thanks for cat introduction Mrs. Langley.

NOT out of sight out of mind

Where's Mum?

She's been gone for hours...

Run, run, run

The lanky legged legend set off today on the beach, or rather mud flat, by the lifeboat station and just kept going and going and going. Fortunately, Daisy stayed in close pursuit but despite screaming at them both, neither was listening. They just kept running.

By this time Walter had managed to prise his HALTI off and it was now dangling by the clip attached to his collar swinging worryingly. The only saving grace being that if it wrapped around his legs it might slow him down. I'd invited my friend to join me on what was meant to be a leisurely stroll; ha, ha, ha - how wrong was I? Even Sophie said she'd never heard me shout so loud. It was a total waste of time - he was FREE.

Eventually with my legs shaking like jelly, my heart pumping and my friend in total shock at his speed, I waited, and he did come back but unless it's in a more contained space he is now GROUNDED!

Different dog!

What's happened to Walter? Despite the rain we set off. My reasoning was that not many people would be out in such foul weather. I was right; we never saw a soul. He trotted through Witch Wood whilst the other two mad brains charged through the mud! You'd never think he'd been a street dog - he sheltered under every bush; he doesn't do wet. Then on to Fairlawn and I let him off. He trotted next to me, had a little sprint and back again. What has happened? I let him stay off his lead all the way to the end and he behaved perfectly. Then we went down onto the beach. Now after Thursday my head said 'don't let

him off,' but my heart said, 'do it'. Big gulp and he was FREE. He was brilliant, sticking close, playing with the girls and coming back when I whistled. I think he's had a brain transplant. It's great.

Through Lytham to the optician who leaves biscuits out for dogs. He sat very politely and waited for his and then we went on to Park View for his final sprint. Again, he came straight back to me.

WHAT HAS HAPPENED?

Another positive day with his highness today

I'm feeling far more settled with him on our walks and let him off to have a sniff around a bit before he chases after me. Park View was the usual chase and try and eat poor Daisy, but now it's a tag team with Walter, Nelly and Daisy getting both barrels.

On to Lytham Hall but I keep his lead on there as there are too many distractions, plus Daisy goes totally bonkers in there and I need to keep her under control. I'm not succeeding!

In Witch Wood we met a beautiful greyhound called Frankie. Walter seemed to quite like her. Usually he shakes and cries when he sees similar dogs to himself, but they appeared happy together.

At Fairlawn Walter played happily. I like it there as it's a little more contained. We did meet another dog and I put Walter back on his lead as he seems to be getting more vocal with other dogs and crouches down as if to play. Or is he going in for the kill? I have no idea but better to be safe than sorry.

Across the park and then home to where a fabulous man was repairing my suite after our chewing session. This man is marvellous; suite repaired, and you can't even tell it had been chewed. And it's been deep cleaned too.

All in a day's work.

Witch Wood

Call the midwife. Or rather the lifeboat!

Today the gang were joined by Joyce Bond on our leisurely (hmmmm) stroll. Joyce is a Walter follower and wanted to meet the lanky legend.

We met on Park View where Daisy greeted with her usual introduction of jumping up and putting muddy paw prints all over Joyce's spotless grey coat. I apologised knowing it wouldn't be the last time, especially as she had brought treats for the gang!

We settled into a muddy trudge in Lytham Hall followed by an even more muddy hike in Witch Wood and then onto Fairlawn where Walter demonstrated how rough he could be with Daisy and showcasing his death rumble in the process. Joyce thought the noise was the diggers working on the sea defence until I told her. It's a horrible rumble!

Then we headed down to the beach. Me being a bit cocky after the past few days let the girls off and then I let Walter go. He ran and ran but instead of running along the shore he ran out to sea. A merry dot on the horizon and I mean dot.

Morning

For the uninitiated, the sea can be miles away at Lytham St Annes, which is precisely where Walter was. I whistled shouted and whistled again. Unable to run, although I wanted to, I started to walk towards him. The shrimpers were watching, and Joyce was yelling too but nothing. Then I realised he had sunk in the mud. The shrimpers asked if I wanted help but that would have frightened Walter, so I stood calling him watching him struggle to pull his long antelope like legs out of the mud. Eventually he was free. He galloped over to me; he was trembling from head to toe and totally covered in mud. In the meantime, Nelly and Daisy were having a ball rolling in the mud and then the sand; totally tarred and feathered.

An hour and a half to clean them. No photos - I was too panic stricken to take any.

Only one thing for it! WINE!

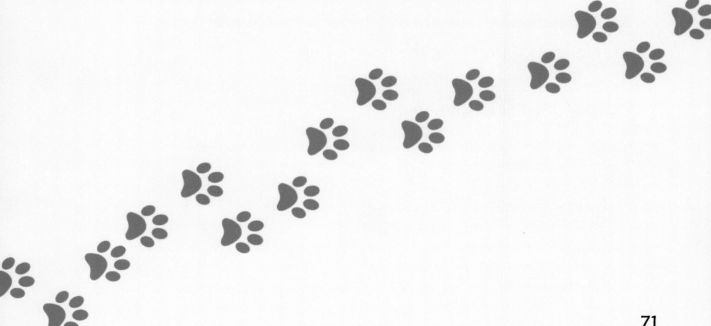

Holey moley

Yes, he's still alive.

Walter has kept a low profile since he ate the chair.

He is a very crafty dog who knows how to wrap us around his little finger or rather his huge gigantic legs.

My husband has spent hours and hours repairing his garden and with the weather so beautiful, spent all day on his knees seeding, re-turfing and planting. Walter helped him.

He lay at the side of my hubby licking his sweaty face. Yuck!

And when he saw him digging he joined in too!

Noooooo! Don't dig the new turf up.

This dog has a death wish.

Chaos

Our walks are going well. He sprints off at break neck speed with Daisy in pursuit but does return, mostly. I spent ages looking for him yesterday. Turned out he was standing next to me camouflaged in the trees. How stupid am I? (Don't answer that).

He was groomed on Friday, he had a lovely bath and smelt divine but oh no, not any longer. Today we had a great walk, running everywhere meeting other dogs; some more scary than others. We went onto the beach. Why are dead porpoises so great to roll on? White blubber stuck to him and the smell was unbelievable! Daisy made a dash for it too but I rugby tackled her to the floor. One stinker is bad enough, but two stinkers is just too many, especially as they both had an appointment at the vet. So, it was home for a quick bath and squirt of nice smelly stuff before we set off to the vet.

Daisy's booster was due, so she raced in to see her favourite receptionist Auntie Jan. She peed all over the floor, her tail going ninety to the dozen and the mop following her close behind. Laid back Walter just took it all in his stride. Rather than stand in Daisy's pee he made himself very comfortable across the reception seats. Daisy was so excited until the needle came out and then the tears and screaming started. Walter was due his booster too, but he still has a castration stitch that's giving him problems. Lifting him onto the table and laying him on his side, legs parted (how amazing is this dog), the lovely vet Fiona started pulling and cutting to try and get the stitches out. I kissed his face and prayed he wouldn't bite me, or my left boob would be a gonna. But not a grumble. Phew!!

Once he'd been pulled about for a while Fiona stopped but Walter remained lying on the table, so he had his injection in this relaxed state. Then he was gently lifted off the table and we headed home.

Nelly had stayed at home as her booster is not due yet, but she was distraught. With both Daisy and Walter gone she was left behind howling the place down. We got home, and she was bouncing around like she was on springs and she raced around the house like a nutter. I'm sure a zoo would be calmer.

Everyone is extremely calm now and all fast asleep. Bliss, total bliss.

I wish could bottle them at these times

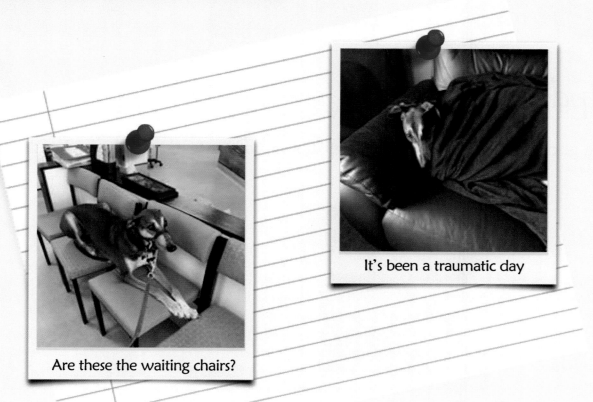

It's been a traumatic day

Are these the waiting chairs?

How cocky are our walks now!

Update...

The good dog has left the building! Walter has just eaten Sophie's Ugg slippers.

Happy Friday

Brilliant walk today

We arranged to meet Sue Sykes and Lucy, one of, if not the biggest follower of Walter. We met on Park View playing fields where, after a mad 10-minute tear around, the gang had expended enough energy to link up with little Lucy and be polite 'ish'. Daisy, who is never polite, jumped all over Sue making her filthy. Into Witch Wood we go, where Sue was very impressed that Walter was off the lead all the time and even more impressed when he came back nearly as impressed as me.

Then onto Fairlawn Road where he galloped off after a golden retriever. When I eventually caught up with him he was having a real rough and tumble in the sand and YES Daisy was in the middle of them both, being flattened! Back through Witch Wood where a school trip of little children, all wearing hi vis jackets, were collecting things. Walter dug his heels in. A bit embarrassing as he was bigger than any of the children and I had to lift him up and carry him past them. No mean feat I can tell you - he is sooooo heavy! He's put on 10 kilos since we found him. I think it's common

knowledge that I am totally nuts.

We came out of the woods and came across two ladies who stopped

me to ask, 'is this Walter, Nelly and Daisy?' I was happy to say 'yes'

although after carrying my big guy in the woods in the rain I looked

a right mess. Why do I never get spoken to when I'm dressed up?

Back across the park where Walter was slowing down and

eventually he stopped.

Life's just great, especially in the sunshine.

Yuck, yuck, yuck!

Today we set off across Park View playing fields about 1:15pm. As we approached the field I saw a little dog, Jack Russell sized. 'Damn,' I thought, I can't let you off Walter.' I was still not sure if he'd eat the little dog. However, the lady was lovely and asked if I usually let mine off. I said that I did, and she said her little pooch was terrified of big dogs so she'd put hers on the lead so mine could go mental. I walked along a little and let the gang off but unbeknown to me the lady also let her little 'Fred??' off too. Next thing I know Fred is making a B line for Walter. OMG please don't kill it, eat it or shake it. Walter went down on his haunches and little Fred ran straight into the side of him. The chase was on. Walter was as good as gold and the lady couldn't believe how unafraid her little dog was. Playtime was perfect.

Onto Witch Wood where, due to his amazing behaviour on the park, I let him stay off the lead all the way, even when other dogs were coming. Another milestone reached?

THEN we hit the beach. Now, I'm trying very hard to take the positives out of this and think that Walter loves me so very much and today he just wanted to prove it by racing along the beach at break neck speed. A seagull flew up and Walter chased it. He ran and ran. Daisy and Nelly were otherwise engaged so this time he was on his own. I blew my whistle, but he was so far away I don't think he could hear it. I stood waving frantically at him. Why did I do that? He was hardly going to wave back was he! He ran to some people and realised it wasn't me, so he swerved away and then spotted me and set off back in my direction.

However, on route back he eyeballed Nelly and Daisy who were very busy. To be honest, I'd been too preoccupied with Walter and wasn't really watching what the other two were getting up to.

Next thing I know, Walter is dragging something across the beach towards me. What the heck had he got? Nelly and Daisy were trying to pull it the other way but NO, Walter really wanted to bring it to me. Thanks a bunch mate. It was a dead black sheep and it was putrid. No wonder the girls had been so quiet! They'd feasted on stinky mutton and trust me their breath stank. What was I going to do with it and them? I shouted at them all to leave which was quite sad as the only one who reacted was Walter rolling into a little ball and shaking. I had to cuddle his stinky face just to get him to move. The girls just looked at me as much as to say how ungrateful are you!

I phoned home to my lovely, patient husband and said, 'please can you run a bath for the dogs; they've found a sheep and are filthy.' To which his response was, 'Des, if you bring a sheep home I'm leaving!' Now there's an idea. After giggling I said, 'don't worry the sheep was dead and the dogs had been eating and rolling on it!'

Bath time is now complete.

I'm in the dog house

The sheep is back there!

Stinky

I got up with a positive spring in my step despite the fact I didn't sleep particularly well. This was due to Walter crushing my chest, Nelly being wrapped around my head on my pillow nose to nose with me and Daisy entwined around my ankles. This seems to be the sleeping pattern the Three Musketeers have settled on and as time goes on I'm getting more and more weary.

After untangling myself, I came downstairs, made a drink and sat in the garden. At 5:30am it was peaceful and beautiful. I flashed up my laptop and I've now written 106 pages of my book. My leading characters are lying around my feet. We've been on an early walk today as Nelly really struggles in the heat and collapses like a star fish in the most awkward of places and then we have to ring for the cavalry (hubby) to rescue us. It happened so many times last summer that £1,800 worth of vet fees later we were told she doesn't like walking when the sun is out. No, I wasn't very popular with my husband, but I think you've already built up a picture that he's hard done by... NOT!

Walter has been a cherub today. We widened the goal posts even further and he was off lead all through Lytham Hall, racing through the trees and generally exploring. He was a bit edgy when he spotted the golfers on the Old Links but he didn't leap onto the course.

As we neared the stinky lake, I put both Daisy and Walter on their leads and let Nelly follow on as 'normally' Nelly is my dream dog. Calm, well behaved, loyal just a total star but NOT today. Straight in the lake she goes. She hates water. OMG, she got out and she was black and stinking. Everyone we saw commented on her appearance and I was paranoid she'd jump up at someone. Not that she ever does, but neither does she jump in lakes! We phoned on ahead to ask for a bucket of hot soapy water to be waiting. There was no way she was going in my bathroom. The black stuff was like tar.

Whilst Walter and Daisy relaxed in the sunshine poor Nelly has been scrubbed to within an inch of her life and to top it all - where has the sun gone?

Best of friends

Boring walk

After a restless night I thought, 'stuff it, let's try again.' Dogs togged up early due to the heat and off we went. I was very tempted to take my taser but, due to the weight of it, I left it on the kitchen table.

Across the park where Daisy's recall appears to have melted with my ice cream. She might as well be sticking her tongue out at me when I call her back, which, in essence, means Walter does the same. If they were little people you could almost hear him say, 'Daisy if you're naughty I will be too.' Nelly is just perfect and never puts a foot wrong. Boy, I tell lies.

Across to Witch Wood where we had a nice walk. The tag team set off chasing something but fortunately caught nothing. Then we made our way down to Fairlawn Road. By this time the sun was getting hot and Nelly procrastinated by laying star fish shape in the shade of a parked car and categorically refused to move. 'Come on poppet,' I encouraged but no. Treats out but no. Dragging no. Only option pick her up and carry her like a baby. Not easy with the tag team in tow but I will not be beaten. I was going to go to the beach but decided the woods would be cooler, so back into Witch Wood where Nelly was happy to walk until they found a convenient watering hole.

I thought the sight hound was the killing machine but oh no, it's Daisy. We have baby robins in the garden and day one out of their nest and devil dog Daisy has eaten one. She is now in total disgrace and has been tied to me all day on Walter's 10 metre training lead. I have been tied in that many knots and Walter, being the tease that he is, keeps trotting past her nose then sprinting off. Daisy tries to catch him but almost gets garrotted and my sun bed surfs across the patio.

Oh well we survived to talk another day... and so will our baby robins. Well what's left of them!

A real 'tree't... fresh water

Let me get to it

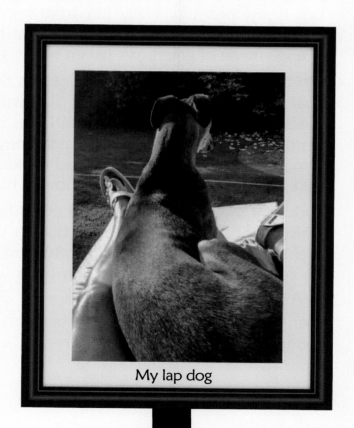

My lap dog

The adventures continue...

I had to go to work this morning, not that I really minded as I love my job but when I finished at 1 o'clock the sun was hiding good and proper. I put my hoody on, put leads on the gang and off we went. Park View is always a good test to see how the rest of the walk is likely to pan out based on their behaviour. Daisy, totally out of control; no recall, chasing birds and butterflies, Walter following Daisy but also desperately sliding along the floor in an attempt to get his HALTI off. Nelly; beautiful Nelly just trotting along behind me, or so I thought, was actually rolling in old grass cuttings that had gone stinky in a pile. She is now a strange shade of green. We haven't even got off the park yet!

On to Witch Wood where the heavens decided to open. Me no coat, Walter no coat and Walter doesn't do wet. Suddenly, a baby rabbit shot out of the bushes. Walter was off. 'Run rabbit, run.' I was screaming at Walter, but he was fixated on the little bunny. Daisy not having any idea why she was sprinting, followed him, barking, but at what she had no idea. The baby bunny ran into the bushes by Lytham Hall School closely followed by Tweedle Dum and Tweedle Dee.

Suddenly there was a bang, and everything stopped. I called but nothing. Then Daisy, very sheepishly came out but no Walter. I called again but nothing. Nelly went in the bush to examine the situation but came out Walterless. Why wouldn't he come out? Then I realised his head was in the railings! Great. B***** great. Now what?

Rain soaked, I crawled into the bush, muttering away to myself. Daisy thinking this was a great game.

The lovely Walter then pulled his head out of the railings and calmly walked out of the bush. However, I couldn't remove myself that easily, partly due to the fact I have a leg that doesn't work as well as it should and doesn't bend, so I had to shuffle out on my bottom. I was now wet and filthy and had three hysterically laughing dogs. Still, off to the beach next - might as well. Damn sheep was still there, only now it's home to several hundred maggots. I did report it to Environmental Health today to ask if they could remove it. None of the dogs wanted to come home. In fact, Daisy was racing around chasing swallows. Only problem with that was that their flight path was Blackpool, so she was going the completely wrong way. Walter was fixated on the damn sheep and the lovely green Nelly was rolling in anything grizzly she could find. I gave up calling them all and sat on the steps leading to the beach, looking like a really sad muppet; filthy and soaked. I think Nelly was the first to feel sorry for me and returned. Next was Walter and finally Daisy.

Hot bath needed and that's just for me. Hubby totally loved it when us lot got home.

Patience of a saint he has.

Wonder what Walter would make of Eeyore

Yum yum; M&S biscuits...

So, it's not all about walks and fun. Tonight, it's about an uncontrollable urge to eat Marks and Spencer's white chocolate cookies. I never eat biscuits but when I do, these are my passion. Sat engrossed in 'Coronation Street' with my biscuit precariously perched in my hand, Walter did a pincer movement across the carpet and, like a Venus flytrap, the biscuit vanished. Knowing he'd done wrong, he then leapt back into his armchair or rather my hubby's armchair that he seems to have commandeered. This is why after 24 years of marriage me and Russ now sit together on the settee each evening. Nelly was on the other settee and Daisy had gone to my bed exhausted.

Not surprising really as the terrible twosome went mud sliding this afternoon. Unfortunately, the tide was out, and the stinky sloppy mud looked so inviting... Thankfully not inviting at all to Nelly. Daisy and Walter raced off until they were mere dots on the horizon. The only way I knew where they were was the sea birds kept flying away; eventually two filthy, happy hounds returned to me.

Russ we're coming home, please prepare the bath AGAIN.

#hesgettingfedupwithme/us

I love those biscuits

Sorry, is this your chair?

OMG

And her too

The angel girl

Football, football, football

Joe, my son, is home for a few days and it's ball skills in the garden. Walter is now a pro when it comes to dribbling but his keepy uppys are miserable and the only way he has total control is by sticking his monster teeth into the ball - game over. Daisy is obviously on the opposite team and relentlessly fouls. Nelly is the referee and has to break the players up.

We had a visitor this afternoon, Craig Marcella. Craig was one of the original Walter hunters and spent many hours looking for him when it was freezing cold back in January. He had to come to see Joe, so we took the opportunity of a catch up with Walter as he'd not seen him since we've had the privileged of adopting him.

I told Walter he had a visitor coming and begged Daisy to behave but not a chance in a million years. I know there's such a thing as poetic licence, but I pull no punches with Daisy; she is totally nuts, bonkers and a thorough embarrassment.

My ball

The gang with Craig

Within five minutes of Craig being here she head butted him in the wrong place which floored him, and he ended up on the ground with Walter. OMG, we need training or shooting. The difference in Walter since Craig last saw him is immense. His calm demeanour and healthy coat are fantastic to see. I'm not adopting any more though! Football on the lawn is a dangerous pastime but we are only brave enough to do it when my hubby goes out. Otherwise we are all dead. Russ has spent hours repairing the lawn after winter madness but even now Walter's rotavator feet churn it up.

Down to the beach this afternoon and that damn sheep is still there! Come on Environmental Health move it, please!

Walter takes off like a bullet only to start dragging the sheep carcass. I'm half tempted to let him give it to Russ as a peace offering but the smell makes me retch.

Fortunately, no bath needed today.

On the head

Easy on a Sunday morning

Sea birds and ducks

Guess where I've been for the last hour? Stuck on the shore line. I've been watching Walter run 50 miles to the left and then 50 miles to the right. OK so slight exaggeration but nevertheless a very long way, chasing birds. His antics, in true Walter fashion, seem to draw a bit of a crowd up on the prom by the Clifton Arms. In fact, the 'twitchers' had trained their binoculars on Walter. At times I wished I'd had some binoculars too! I blew my whistle. Useless thing. Nelly came but then again, she was walking right behind me; darling dog. Daisy looked up but gave me that look that says, 'I'll come when he does.' Walter's response from afar was apparently, 'get stuffed, I'm having way too much fun.' In the sea, running through chest deep mud, birds fleeing for their lives. Two ducks just relaxing in the sunshine had to fly off rapidly when rudely interrupted by a lanky legged maniac. He'll tire out soon or so I thought, but oh no, not today. Far too much energy. Eventually Daisy the Duracell dog returned to me covered in mud, with her tongue lolling from her mouth, to flop at my feet. I blew my whistle again in the direction of Southport where he was heading, and OMG Walter lifted his head and set off back in my direction. I held my breath. Surely, he'd get distracted on route? But no, he kept coming and then to top it off, when he got to me, he sat at my feet. How embarrassing, people on the prom were clapping enthusiastically. Whilst I should have turned and taken a bow, I didn't want to let them see how much I was shaking. I really thought he'd gone.

We climbed the steps up onto the prom and a lady and her husband said, 'that was amazing. He is so fast, but you kept him focused with the whistle and then he returned.' To be honest, I was totally amazed he came back too. I was honest and said that to them and we laughed.

Just hosed Daisy and Walter down in the garden. Neither were too impressed. Nelly sat on my sun bed just watching the debacle.

Another day, another walk in the 'life of Riley'.

92

Filthy on cream chair... lovely

My angel

Dreaming of birds

93

Squirrels

Our walk had to be later than usual today and by the time I got in at 4:30pm instead of 1pm, the hounds were going mental. Although my hubby has been at home all day with them, it's me they want.

We set off across Park View; perfect. Along Fairlawn; perfect. Then it was decision time. Do I go down to the beach or back through the woods? All three dogs were spotless and I'm a bit too weary to be bathing dogs now and tea needs cooking, so I opted for the woods.

Breakfast on the terrace

I let them all off their leads. Angel Nelly was transfixed with her new pink ball. Daisy, being Daisy, was trying desperately to steal it so she could ruin Nelly's day and Walter was... Well where was Walter? I doubled back calling for Walter, and then this noise erupted from the bushes. It was a cross between a strangled howl and a cheer! What on earth?

The squirrel!

Nelly: 'I'm disgusted with you two'

I set off at a trot; not easy when you're disabled. And there he was... with a squirrel in his mouth! OMG. 'Drop it,' I shouted. He did, and Daisy grabbed it! I grabbed her, and she dropped it.

Nelly just watched, bemused by the commotion. The poor squirrel was barely alive, and I was willing it to die so it didn't suffer anymore. I kept the dogs on their leads, not Nelly she didn't need it, and walked away. When I was a good distance away I let them off. Daisy I swear whispered to Walter 'NOW,' and they both spun round and raced back to the squirrel. Next thing I know they brought me half a squirrel each.

With me heaving in a bush and Nelly just sat with her pink ball, I had to pull myself together catch the killers and come home.

Suddenly Russ's lasagne doesn't look too appealing!

Bugs

Life was calm in the Riley household. All my family together for a change.

Sat chatting in the lounge, telly on. Walter commandeering the 'master's'

armchair, the rest of us squashed onto settees, Nelly and Daisy comfy on

the floor.

Out of the blue Walter dived off the chair leapt about 10 foot in the air.

OK slight exaggeration. We had a fly in the room! The whole family just

sat for a minute, mouths open not really registering what was going on.

Nelly and Daisy continued resting, oblivious. Despite a valiant effort, the

fly escaped. But that didn't faze Walter; he was off. Now my lounge

is only little, and Walter is a solid lump of lankiness and he was throwing

himself around the room. My 'happy' hubby dived in front of the TV

before that went for a burton; I protected my crystal cabinet and the kids

were poleaxed on the floor. Walter now feet up on the windowsill, jaws

chomping and then it was over as quickly as it had started. Fly devoured.

Walter was again happy and took up residence in the arm chair. Nelly

and Daisy had not budged an inch during the commotion.

My house is NUTS.

Mmmm tasty

Life of Riley

When I watch Walter 'playing' in the garden, either with Daisy or a ball I realise what a massive road he's been on.

We've had the lanky legend just over four months and he is the happiest dog ever. When we rescued him, he was a skinny, scabby hound with lots of sores, ears were covered in scabs and a twig embedded in his head! The running machine is now in tip top condition. The girls adore him, mainly because every night their evening meal consists of fish and olive oil! Walter's coat is gleaming, Nelly's is thick and luxurious and if Daisy would stop digging long enough, she too would look glam.

Every day is an adventure. Yes, that's one way of putting it. We're having to keep to the woods at the moment as it's so hot when I finish work. Apart from Daisy, they are a dream; trotting along in the undergrowth or beside me. Most of the time Daisy is digging holes, chewing plants, trying to climb trees, jumping up people in cream chinos and generally being a nightmare.

There is no food aggression and musical chairs with food bowls is quite common. After living feral, things could have been horribly different. I daren't say he's stopped eating the furniture but then why would he bother chewing leather when there's a BBQ most evenings?

At TV time he takes the 'master's' chair and at bed time he commands the most space.

WALTER definitely has the LIFE OF RILEY.

Guess what?

Devil dog and her mate are at it again. Hubby and my son are out on the golf course. Daisy has felled a dead branch - from where I have no idea.

And so, the game begins.

Today, 'happy hubby' has been lopping trees. The gang are in their element!

Beautiful weather. Obviously paddling pool time. This is a first for lanky.

Dazed and bemused

The gang have, for once been extremely well behaved and, with the weather being so warm, our walks have been at obscure times of the day. One minute they are relaxing on my bed just getting ready to take on the day, when next thing they know I'm dragging them out or at the other end of the day, just when they think it's bedtime, it's off we go for walkies. Totally bewildered!

A couple of times the tide has been in and the three musketeers have wallowed like a heard of hippos in the beautiful dirty, thick, muddy water. It's the birds that I'm learning to hate. How long can Walter chase them for? And if he thinks I'm wading knee deep in mud he can think again. Unfortunately, Nelly and Daisy don't have legs like a giraffe, so they end up neck high in said mud. OMG they are absolutely filthy and as we walk past the designer eating establishments of Lytham, people either recoil in horror or laugh at us. Walter holds his head up high and carries on, Nelly trudges behind too hot and wearing a mud pack and Daisy, hmmmm Daisy slides her face along the pavement, shakes and splatters people as she walks, and makes a bee line for the smartest person she can find to try and jump up at them. She really needs shooting.

We stop at the opticians for a biscuit. Three a day - I think I'm going to have to contribute soon! Next to 'Le Roti' for the best tasting water in Lytham. The staff there really spoil us and then home to the waiting sprinkler/hose pipe.

Breakfast in bed.... enjoy your day

Games and antics

I've invested in a camera, so I can watch the dogs when we're not at home and talk to them; or shout at them if they're being naughty! I've been off work the past few days which has been fantastic as I've been at home all day with my 'merry band of men'. Well that's not strictly true as Nelly and Daisy are women. However, we've all been together.

Hubby has been away and returns tonight. This morning meant I had to leave them home alone for a few hours. With the carefree attitude that I seem to have adopted with Walter, I left for work knowing the leather sofa repair man is on speed dial. The house is spotless, and the garden is looking great; let's hope it is when I get home.

I got into work turned my phone into camera mode and immediately Walter popped up on the screen. Bless him he was lying in his bed, not a care in the world. Next, I pan around the room and princess Nelly is spread eagled in the armchair. But where is Daisy? As if by magic she trots in front of the camera… carrying a rhododendron bush! I can talk to them through the camera so stupidly I shout, 'NO DAISY,' at which Walter leaps out of his bed barking profusely at the camera. Nelly doesn't move.

I returned home at 1pm to a hall full of twigs and mud, and a toilet roll shredded on the stairs but nothing else. How fabulous have they been? I can't wait to spy on my hubby when he comes home; he doesn't know I've got this new camera!

This afternoon has been another warm one, so I took the pack down to the beach. The grass is so long it's a work out in its self, especially for Daisy's little legs. Nelly stays with me; honestly, she is a dream dog!

We managed to stay remarkably clean as well, so no hose pipe required. All in all, a very easy day. Hubby, or Mrs Doubtfire as I like to call him, is back tonight so normal (chaotic) service will be resumed. I'm glad as to be honest I'm sick of watering the b***** garden.

What a strange day!

The gang and me set off for our daily constitutional across Park View and into a battered Witch Wood. Last night's wind had certainly had its say on the trees. There were leaves and branches everywhere. Daisy was in her element dragging, what I'd like to say were twigs but they were more like logs, along with her, taking my legs out on more than one occasion. Then down to the back of Fairlawn where I could see the tide was in, so we headed to the beach.

Desperate for playtime, I let them off and two of them (no guesses for which two) bolted to the water, whilst angel dog stayed with me. The two nutters in the camp we're having a fine time charging in and out of the water. I think at one point, Walter did try and hold Daisy's head under the water, but she popped up like a cork ready to fight some more. Nelly In the meantime was happy paddling in a puddle next to me!

Another day in paradise

It's funny when I look back and remember how uncertain we were about Walter's behaviour and someone said I'd have to walk Walter separately to the other two as he would always be too rough. I remember thinking at the time, 'well that's not going to happen, he'll have to learn.' I'd like to say it's down to my first-class training, but I couldn't train anything, not even my hubby (he's great). Daisy likes a bit of rough and he's certainly that, but they absolutely adore each other, and there is no way could we separate them. Even Nelly wakes up in the morning with her arms resting upon him.

106

From the beach we headed back through Lytham where we were confronted by a group of people carrying clip boards. A man stopped me and said they were on a treasure hunt and could they borrow a dog for a short walk video. I said that providing they didn't run off with him, they could use Walter. However, Walter had other ideas and when the man took the lead Walter grumbled. It's a bit like a death rattle and the man said he'd prefer to use the little black dog. Is he mad? He bent down to stroke Daisy just as she jumped up! I think Daisy broke his nose. Eventually a lady from the group stepped forward and got a video with Angel Nelly. How easy was that!

Then home, where we all crashed out in the garden. Thank goodness the sun has come out.

Another day in paradise for the three amigos.

Angel dog

Daisy, don't bite my ear; I just want to relax

The heat has beaten her; she's quiet.

Our 'hot dog'.... doesn't need a BBQ

Can I have the wet towel now please?

It's amazing what a bit of love can do. Six months ago, if I got my hoover out the 'lanky Lytham legend' would howl like a werewolf and shake like a jelly. Now he uses it to lull himself to sleep. The other two don't mind it either.

Just as well really as I love my hoover.

What an odd day!

For fear of boring you about Walter's antics, I've cut the updates down. To be honest he has settled so well that apart from digging up the garden and being followed around by my hubby spraying all his flowers with anti-chew spray, he is being well behaved. The anti-chew spray does not work!

Today though has been odd! We set off for our walk as normal and everything was going great. We went through Witch Wood which was uneventful and then we went down to Seafield Road where Gypsies have set up camp on the football pitches. There are about eight caravans, kids and lots of tied up dogs, mainly French Bulldogs, many looking like they'd just had puppies. Walter was terrified. His tail vanished between his legs and the cowering started. I'm not sure what was going through his head, but he would not move. With Daisy also refusing to move because her mate wouldn't, and Nelly sat patiently waiting for the two goons to sort themselves out, I had a problem. Despite whispering sweet nothings in his ear, he was staying put. Too big to carry and too stubborn to move, I had to think creatively. Hmmm I know kidnap Daisy! I scooped her up, got Nelly moving and hoped Walter would follow. It worked and like an Exocet missile he shot passed the field. It was truly horrible to see him so frightened.

We went to the beach where Walter expended all of his pent-up energy by rolling Daisy in the sand like a sausage roll.

On the way home we went onto Lytham Green where we found two sheep dogs locked in a pick-up truck. There was just a tiny gap open in the window and a bowl of water.

A lovely trainee PCSO came to assist. As I have little hands I was able to squeeze my arm through the window, hoping it wouldn't be bitten off, to prise it open. Thank God for my gang's treats. Although they weren't impressed having been in the truck almost two hours and with another hour and half left on the ticket, we were deciding how to get the dogs out. A lovely lady brought my three some water, of which I pinched a bit. Just as we were about to hatch our rescue plan, Garry the Senior PCSO arrived on the scene along with the owner who looked very sheepish. I wanted to full on punch him but thought better of it as who'd look after my gang if I was inside?

My hubby has absolutely no idea how close he was to having another two new lodgers, which bearing in mind what angel dog (not the terrible two) has done since I got home is probably just as well! I didn't like that bush anyway!

Oh no! Nelly's ripping 'his' plants out now!

Hi vis jackets are a no no

We were walking through Witch Wood today when a poor unsuspecting man walking in a hi vis jacket walked past the three amigos and me. 'Good morning,' said I. Nelly completely ignored him, Daisy got between his legs and almost tripped him up and Walter... well he had other ideas!

Obviously, these jackets mean something to Walter, but I have no idea what. He spun around, raced up behind the man giving his death rattle. The man stopped, turned around and Walter stopped dead in his tracks. My heart had stopped too by this time. For one awful minute I thought Walter was going to jump on him, but thankfully he came to his senses in time. I don't think the man realised how close he had come to being flattened. He just said, 'gosh that noise made me jump!' I tried to look calm and collected but my insides were doing back flips. That's something else to be aware of in the life with Walter.

Tonight is my daughter's birthday gathering. She is now 23; where have the years gone? Walter has spent most of the afternoon preening himself in preparation for her guests. The fruit punch is chilling in the fridge and the beer pong is set up in the garden. It could get messy! I will be on the alert this time because last time my kids had a party I'm sure Walter was mine sweeping the glasses as he was very subdued the next day. I'm assuming he had a massive hangover. Nelly is more sensible and takes water with hers, and Daisy - God knows where she'll be; probably dancing on the tables.

Morning! It's great to be alive

Rushy, rushy day

Today I was up at 5am as it's my daughter's official birthday. I jumped in my car, in my nightie but unfortunately not under the cover of darkness! I drove to her boyfriend's house where I decorated her car in helium balloons, as she has an induction day for her new job and has to leave at 7am. I give a quick 'good morning' to the neighbour. I was praying I'd see no one but in true RILEY fashion, hold your head up and pretend you regularly go out in your nightie and slippers.

I got back home where the three amigos were not impressed I had gone out without giving them breakfast first. So, bark and howl the house down waking the 'grinch', oops I mean my hubby, in the process. Then I had a quick shower and was off to work.

Fast forward and out for our daily constitutional. Unfortunately, a Boxer took a dislike to Walter and tried to bite him, but Daisy was having none of it. Whilst Walter trembled like a jelly, Daisy went for the Boxer's back leg - I don't think she could reach anything else! However, it worked. The lady owner was very apologetic, and we had a little chat, obviously about Walter.

After that we went down to the beach where the tide was in. No need for swimming costumes, straight in the water all three of them. Obviously, Walter went the furthest as he has longest legs. Daisy tried to keep up but needed a snorkel! Nelly just paddled.

After racing about through the marshes, making sure they were not only filthy but were stinky too, we trotted through Lytham to the opticians for our daily biscuits.

A nice 'thank you' and then to Le Roti for our afternoon drink, at which point we met the lovely Anne Turner, another avid Walter follower. She popped her head out of Dunderdale's estate agents to enquire if this stinky lump (my words) was Walter. I said, 'yes' and then to my horror I saw that she was wearing very smart white trousers! Nooo; not with Daisy. I had visions of her going back inside with slimy mud stains down the front of her previously pristine white trousers. Shortening Daisy's lead to about two inches, almost garrotting her in the process, we had a brief chat and then we carried on. Walter has touched so many people that my walks are a real pleasure.

We got home, I had a quick change and went to Bradford to watch my son play his first home match for his new team Bradford City FC against Sheffield United. Proud moment.

Great day but a bit weary.

Where's our breakfast?

Oh no... having been at a medical appointment all day in Manchester and not being able to go out with the dogs, Walter has let me know he's not happy by eating my furniture ... AGAIN!

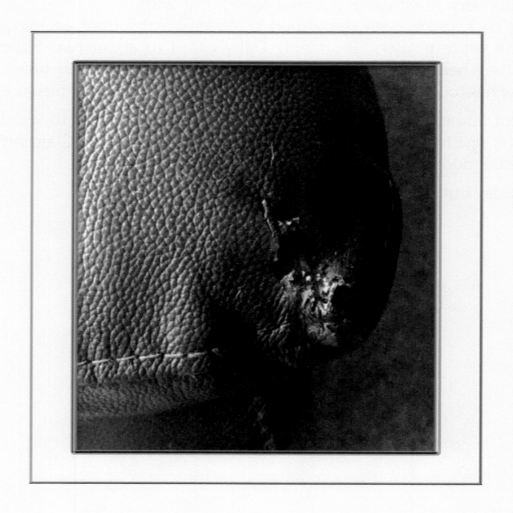

Gardening

Today has been all about reshaping and repairing the garden! Boring.

After spending quite a lot of money on plants and shrubs, Walter and Daisy, but not angel dog Nelly, have either trampled, squashed or wee'd all over them, leaving us with just a soil bed instead of a flower bed. As you know my hubby is obsessed with his b****** garden.

Today we went and bought pebbles and huge pots. Walter will have to aim high to pee on these and the flowers. We will not be beaten.

On the hottest day of the year so far, I have been humping soil and plant pots. It would appear I'm the humper and hubby is the technical director. I'll change it when he goes out later. So far, so good but quite a long way to go yet.

We are going out much later tonight as it is so warm, but Walter has the devil in him today, so I think I could be in for a rocky ride. In other words, Lytham, be prepared!

RADA

What an absolute diva Walter is!

Dodging the rain this morning, we set off for our daily constitutional. Today we went through Lytham and down towards the lifeboat station. The three amigos were all playing nicely, having their usual rough and tumble in the long grass, when suddenly Walter's nose went up in the air and he was off. To be honest, I really thought this was it! He ran and ran; past the sea defence work without stopping to read that he wasn't allowed and carried on. Totally out of sight. Trying to encourage Nelly to get a spurt on isn't easy, so we ambled down towards Fairhaven Lake. I blew and blew my whistle but nothing; he was having way too much fun chasing herons and they weren't helping me either. Suddenly Walter changed direction and was sprinting back to me, or so I thought. Wrong! He went straight past me and back to Lytham. There was no way Nelly was going back to Lytham again, so we sat on the sand and waited. And waited and waited. After about an hour Walter thought he'd better come back. Little monkey.

Quickly on his lead and one extremely dirty dog was being taken back home in disgrace. We had been walking for a short time when suddenly Walter let out this piercing howl, lifted his right front leg in the air and collapsed on the floor in a heap. I had no idea what had happened, but he was screaming. A man came rushing out of 'The Taps' pub to ask me if my dog had been hit by a car. I said, 'no', but it sounded more like he'd been run over by a steam roller. I couldn't see anything in his foot but if I touched it he screamed louder. Nelly just pretended she wasn't with us and Daisy thought it was great fun and tried to bite his other leg whilst it was in the air.

Total chaos. The helpful man vanished. I got a tissue out of my pocket but had no water, so next best thing - I spat on his foot. I rubbed a little having seen that it's what they always do at football matches with the magic sponge, and hey ho Walter sprung to his feet and we were off. I have no idea what actually occurred today.

We trotted home at a brisk pace and waited for our lovely groomer to titivate the gang.

They are now fast asleep. I won't be long either.

The invalid

This dog exhausts me

Angel dog

School holidays

'Enjoy the six weeks school holidays,' my colleagues said, 'doing anything nice?' Are they mad? I've got Walter. Nuff said.

This morning started with a trip to the vets with Nelly for her annual injections. With that, plus three worming tablets and three flea treatments, I need a lie down. However, we headed off to the opticians. More a necessity than glamour, especially as yesterday I spent ages whistling at a seagull in the distance thinking it was Walter. The fact it was a seagull explained why it ignored me for almost 40 minutes before I realised Walter was actually 'eating' Daisy behind me. The lovely man at Lytham Eyewear Opticians spent ages with me and eventually I left with new glasses and contact lenses ordered. I've never tried contact lenses before. Another big bill; good job my hubby is away!

Now it's a really good job my hubby is away as I've adopted two more animals today; Fred and Ginger. Hubby's only been gone 24 hours and the likelihood is he won't return when he finds out. One can hope. Only joking; he's lovely really. So, this was the scenario. My lovely Dad was given fish by each of his grandchildren on his 80th birthday. So, he had four fish in total. Two of them died; not sure whose two but he was left with two. They grew rather large. Now my Mum and Dad have lovingly cared for Fred and Ginger but 10 years on, it's getting a bit much; well keeping them clean is. They bought this gadget to help them, but you have to suck on a pipe to start the water flowing and I think 10 years of swallowing fish poo has had its toll, although their complexions are unbelievable and their hair very curly.

Anyway, last night Dad phoned me to ask if I knew anyone who would give them a good home. Haha. ME. So, trip to Pets at Home this afternoon, designer fish tank purchased as well as plants and rocks. More money not to mention the power socket I've had to run for the filter and the light. Thank goodness 'he's' away.

Just returned from a restful dog walk with three hot doggies who are now transfixed watching the fish in the hall. I can watch TV in peace tonight then.

Perfect.

Fred & Ginger arrive

The dying swan...

Nelly, angel dog, really let the side down today.

We set off earlier than normal for our walk as hubby is back this afternoon from his jaunt and I need to introduce him to our new residents, who by the way, had a good night's sleep once I'd sussed out their night light. Nelly is not too keen on rain nor sunshine to be honest. In fact, I think it's fair to say that apart from sitting on my lap, she's not keen on much. We walked across the park. Walter and Daisy were tearing about like idiots and then we crossed over Ballam Road towards Witch Wood. Nelly dug her heels in, lay down on the grass verge and refused to move. I was actually talking to my Mum on the phone at the time, giving her an update on their fish, when Nelly lay down and, tug as I might, she wouldn't get up. Next, she lay on her side looking like she was dead. A car drove past us and then reversed back up the road. Two lovely ladies asked if she was OK. At the thought she might be in with a lift, Nelly sprung to her feet, only for the very kind ladies to drive away laughing.

Into the woods where they all ran about doing their own thing. Walter and Daisy foraging for critters and Nelly just happy to chase her little ball.

On to the beach where the lanky legend exploded into full flight, but I capped him before he went too far as I needed to get home and head my hubby off before he met Fred and Ginger.

Going back through Lytham where Nelly decided to throw her dying swan act again, only this time it was right outside Stringers Department Store door. Despite me telling worried pedestrians she was fine she just lay on the pavement.

Oh No! The Police stopped in a van. Now we were drawing attention to ourselves. I explained Nelly was fine it was just a foible of hers, but I could tell the policeman was unsure. So, I took out her little ball and up she jumped. I've had to bounce the ball all the way home!

Hubby is back but suddenly Fred is not looking too well. He's kind of floating near the bottom of the very expensive tank. I phoned my Mum but apparently Fred's a pensioner and likes a doze in the afternoon. Personally, I think it's a bit more serious. Also, on closer inspection they appeared to have cataracts. Maybe they need to go to the optician!

Only in my house could these things happen!

Nelly flop 1

Nelly flop 2

Hot, hot, hot...

We haven't been out today, yet! Just too hot. The three amigos have flopped around the garden, drunk lots of water and peed over everything that moves, including my sunbed. Walter!

I left them in the hands of my daughter all day yesterday whilst I went to Shrewsbury to watch my son in a football match. Bradford City won. Sophie wasn't impressed at being left in charge of the dogs.

Unfortunately, Fred and Ginger are not doing too well. Actually, that's not strictly true as Ginger's fine; it's Fred. He's still floating near the bottom. Now being the nut that I am I've been to the fish doctor today and apparently Fred looks to be constipated (bladder bloat). Explain that to my hubby. £20 later and we had medicine to administer. I was panicking that I'd have to get tablets down his throat and I was so relieved to find out it was three syringes full of liquid to add to the water. I've done as I'm told but no miracle yet. I'll keep you posted.

Only we could get constipated fish!

An up and down day!

The day didn't get off to the best start. Unfortunately, Fred, the geriatric goldfish, took a turn for the worse last night.

Despite buying constipation medicine Fred appeared to be struggling to breathe. I moved him into an isolation tank but by this morning he was gasping. I phoned my lovely vets 'Greenways' and arranged to take him in. So, with my daughter driving, as trying to drive the car with a goldfish bucket between your knees isn't easy we arrived at the vets. Unfortunately, Fiona told me what I already thought and poor Fred was humanely euthanised. RIP Fred. Mum and Dad had him for 10 years. I had him a week and he died!

Next, we went out for a walk. Nelly poleaxed on the floor; too hot for her. Walter and Daisy were tearing around like mad men. Unfortunately, at Park View a man was praying on his prayer mat just as we decided to cross. I spotted him too late! Daisy raced over and tried to pull the tassels on his mat. As you know, I am unable to run due to a stiff leg but 'Jake the peg' had nothing on me! I apologised profusely to the man, but he stayed in the zone'.

Then we went to the opticians for contact lenses so that when Walter sprints off I can see him, even when it's raining. Mark in Lytham Eyewear couldn't have been more patient. Lenses in no problem - great I can see. Lenses out - not a chance. Try as I might I could not get them out. I now look like I've been crying for a year and my skin is baggier than normal where I've pulled my eyeball socket down. Not a good look when your hubby says 'let's go out for dinner.'

Fred's final resting place

Too hot for Nelly

What a doggie day!

Walter, Daisy, Nelly and Lucy set off for a 'leisurely' stroll. Yes, we had a new member in our gang today.

We met Sue Sykes, one of the original Walter brigade, on Park View as she needed a Walter fix. I think it's safe to say that she now needs a lie down instead. Everything was great. I made a decision to let Walter off his HALTI to see if he'd pull me over or, worse still, use the fact he could open his mouth wider to eat something or someone. Sue saw first-hand how popular Walter is with people stopping to chat all the way through the woods. The lanky legend sucked in all the attention whilst Daisy jumped all over anyone who gave attention to Walter and not her. Nelly lay in the mud and little Lucy, at 13 years old, trotted along beside Sue. So well behaved. Show off.

We went down to Fairlawn where they mingled with other hounds and then we moved on to the beach.

Walter, Walter, Walter; you are such a pain. The tide was in and more importantly so were the b***** seagulls. It was feet on the starting blocks, lead off and 'see ya'. He was off. It's a little disconcerting when you notice a man watching him through binoculars. Yes, that's how far away he was. I blew on the blessed whistle I keep around my neck but, to be honest, he was so far away I didn't know if he could hear or see me or Sue.

I was a little concerned, Sue was very concerned. The man with the binoculars commented how every time I blew the whistle he looked up. Walter, never mind look back; how about come back? Not a chance; Walter has his own agenda on our walks!

In the meantime, Daisy, Nelly and Lucy were paddling in a little puddle at the side of us. Even Daisy was not impressed with Walter's behaviour today. Oh wait. He's coming back covered in mud, soaking wet, smiling and not even out of breath. The binocular man stated the obvious, 'gosh he can run!' I KNOW THAT!!!

We are home now. Sue's gone home for a rest and Walter is resting too.

To be continued…